THE INNOCENT
YET DEAD
WHY??

THE INNOCENT YET DEAD WHY??

Edward J. Hayes

To order additional copies of this book, contact:
Xlibris
1-888-795-4274
www.Xlibris.com
Orders@Xlibris.com
806292

Contents

PREFACE

WE MUST CONFRONT OUR PAST AND
THE REALITY OF THE PRESENT

The disproportionate killing of black people is not a new phenomenon. Even though it was not until 1991 when the first public beating – post-civil rights era – was captured on camera (Rodney King), the historical evidence of public harming and devaluing of black bodies dates to enslavement, and was reinforced in the 19th century when lynching laws were in place. In a lot of ways, police brutality against black people mirrors lynching. Today blacks, Latinos, and Native Americans are disproportionately killed by the police should come as no surprise given that policing in the U.S. has its origins in the mission to conquer Native Americans and then to prevent enslaved Africans from fleeing.

No matter how uncomfortable it makes us feel, we should frame police brutality against people of color as a structural racism and white supremacy problem. It is not simply the fault of individual ill-intentioned, racist, power-hungry, authority-abusing officers. It goes much further and deeper than that.

Time to stop the rotation in search of an answer that really lies in a preventable cause of death. One that makes us all uncomfortable to address – racism.

ACKNOWLEDGEMENTS

It is very important that I recognize and thank my Lord and Savior Jesus Christ for giving me the time, courage, motivation, determination, and drive to complete this book. Without His mercy, this would not have come to fruition.

To Jackie, my wife, life companion, and best friend for her encouragement and excellent proof reading which were a tremendous help that improved the readability and clarity for the contents of the book.

To Dr. Everett Penn for the many hours of rich dialogue on determining the content of the book along with the many enjoyable lunches we shared during the project. His expertise in the area of criminal justice proved to be extremely valuable in shaping the final product.

Also, many thanks to Marie Best for her initial typing of the first draft of the book, as well as tremendous gratitude to Gigi Daniels for her unstinting efforts to complete revision after revision to get the final document finished. Her critical eye and suggestions for improvement of the book are truly appreciated.

Finally, to the late Steven Hayes my brother, whose murder provided the initial concern, motivation, and determination to take on the challenge of writing this book. **Rest in peace my brother.**

Edward J. Hayes

INTRODUCTION

July 2011 my only brother was tazed four times by Webster policemen, became unconscious, and never recovered from the tazing which eventually killed him. My brother suffered from being bipolar, a terrible mental illness which causes huge swings in behavior; from being highly motivated to action, to very low/deep depression. His typical behavior when having an episode was to yell and ask "Why, why is this happening," and to bang tables, desk, cars, etc. with his fists. His last and fatal episode occurred at the Nassau Bay Hilton, TX where he was treated inhumanely by police, tazing him numerous times, which eventually led to his death.

The physicians who treated him before death constantly raised the question, why was he treated in such an inhumane manner? I also asked myself the same question and could only conclude that he was killed because he was a large black man whom the police were afraid. He was UNARMED, shirtless, with hands in view, yet three to five policemen chose to taze him to death, rather than to utilize other methods to subdue him. Serve and protect? Rather, I say police through-out America serve and kill mainly black and other minority persons, a la Trevor Martin, Michael Brown and Eric Gardner; just to mention a few other such murders or killings without any apparent accountability for such horrible behaviors on the part of law enforcement officers.

The outrageous number of such police actions is appalling and just another form of public lynchings that continue to occur when a segment of the population has its freedom abrogated, as is the freedom of blacks and minorities in the good old USA today.

Yes, the land of the free. Clearly, being raised in a small Southern town in the 1950's and 60's had a major impact on my views and beliefs about police actions towards people of color then and now. I must say, during those days we as black people knew what to expect from white policemen and we were prepared and took appropriate actions to avoid any unwanted confrontation. This is not the case today. In later years, black people have been lulled into a false sense of equality and freedom. Clearly, in many instances such beliefs are detrimental to our well-being and leads to murder. Laws have changed in America since the 1950's. Later President Obama was elected, but America is still racist at its core and has not yet accepted its changing diverse population. What a pity, and shame on us as a nation for our lack of acceptance of the new demo- graphic. I ache inside about my brother's death, yet I feel even worse at the rise of conservatism and overt white supremacy in our country and the efforts to enforce more control over people of color each and every day. The future for us as a nation seems glum unless significant national and state policy changes are made to address and correct the numerous injustices that plague our nation relative to police killings, of not only people of color, but innocent citizens of all races as well.

MacDonald (30) suggested that every unjustified police shooting of a law abiding citizen is a terrible tragedy. Given the appalling history of racism in this country and the complicity of police on that history, police shootings of black men are particularly and understandable fraught. Police training must work incessantly to eliminate all unjustified uses of lethal force and make sure that officers treat EVERYONE they encounter with courtesy and respect within the confines of the law. Drawn weapons with the intention to kill should not be the first option.

The abuse and killing of people of color and specifically black people in America between 1999 and 2018 by police/law enforcement have again risen to the attention of the national and international audience. As a result, the American Judicial system and its handling of such killings may undermine the

American System of democracy as we know it and represent it to the world. Although the recent attention to such killings and abuse without accountability for law enforcement during the years 1998-2018, it is important to recognize that the problem dates back as early as 1955 when Emmett Till, a 14-year-old black teenager was lynched in Mississippi after being falsely accused of flirting with a white woman. The brutality of his murder and the fact that his killers were acquitted drew worldwide attention to the long history of violent abuse and persecution of blacks in America without typical consequences. Additionally, in March 1994, Rodney King, a black taxi driver was brutally kicked and beaten by Los Angeles Police Department Officers following a high-speed car chase. Much of the beating was videotaped and sent to local news station KTLA. The video shows four officers surrounding King, several of them striking and kicking him repeatedly, while other officers stood by doing nothing. Parts of the footage were shown worldwide and raised public concern about police treatment of minorities in America.

The purpose of this book is to show the consistency of continued abuse and killings of Blacks by Law enforcement and the undeniable lack of punishment or accountability of such treatment in many instances; secondly, to provide a summary and outcomes of some of the killings that drew national media attention; thirdly, to offer suggestions for improving the relationship between law enforcement and minority communities; and finally, to offer suggestions for systematic changes to prevent the lack of accountability for such killings in America. It is critically important for policemen, sheriffs, deputies, constables, prosecutors, and judges to realize that there is little hatred of them across the Whites, Blacks, and Latinos. There are various levels of mistrust among these groups, but no research that documents wide levels of hate. Bridging the trust gap is one of the outcomes that will come from this book, as well as some guidelines that may pave the way for better relationships between law enforcement and Black, Latino and White communities.

PART I

THE ISSUES AND CONCERNS

1. THE CONTINUED ABUSE

The Washington Post (2015) conducted an analysis of fatal shootings by on duty police officers that clearly showed among the thousands of fatal shootings at the hand of police since 2005, ONLY 54 officers have been charged. MOST WERE CLEARED OR ACQUITTED IN THE CASES THAT WERE RESOLVED. The analysis was based on a wide range of public records and interviews with law enforcement, judicial and other legal experts and sought to identify for the first time every officer who faced charges for such shootings since 2005. It is noteworthy that these cases represent only a small fraction of the thousands of fatal police shootings that occurred during that time period of history in America. In an overwhelming majority of the cases where an officer was charged, the PERSON KILLED was UNARMED. The Washington Post analysis found where prosecutors pressed charges, there were typically other factors that made the case exceptional, which included: a victim shot in the back, a video recording of the incident, incriminating testimony from other officers or allegations of a cover-up. Forty-three such cases involved at least one of the above factors, and nineteen cases involved at least two. Also, according to the analysis, the officers that were charged since 2005 for fatal shootings, more than three fourth, 75% were white and two thirds of their victims were minorities, all but two were black. Nearly all of the other cases involved black officers who killed black victims. In one other instance, a Latino officer shot a white person, and in another an Asian officer killed a black person. Undoubtedly, identifying the exact role race plays as a determining factor in such fatal shootings and prosecutions are very difficult. Sometimes prosecutors sought charges in an atmosphere of protesting individuals who accuse police of racism. Race also appeared to be a factor in court cases when federal prosecutors filed charges against officers for allegedly violating victim's civil rights. Six white officers faced federal civil rights charges for killing blacks. Prosecutors across the nation deny that race is a factor in their decisions to bring charges against officers. Most indicated they pursued cases based on legal merits. But Defense Lawyer Doug Friesen who represented a white officer convicted in 2013 [41] for fatally shooting an unarmed black man stated emphatically "It would be naïve for a prosecutor to say race is not a consideration in such cases".

2. THE PERCEPTION OF INJUSTICE

Research demonstrates that most police officers who killed people are white and most of the victims are black. The Washington Post analysis (2015) showed that 75% of the reviewed fatal cases, the officer was white and of those, two thirds of those shot and killed were a black person. In none of the cases did a black officer fatally shoot a white person. Unfortunately, in most cases, prosecutors fail to press charges against police even if there were strong suspicions that an officer had committed a crime. Prosecutors will tell you that it takes compelling proof that at the time of the shooting the victim did not pose a threat either to the officer or to bystanders. THEREIN LIES THE RUB. Why is the officer empowered to have such life and death decision making authority regarding imminent threat to himself and others, even if such threat were determined; why must the officer resort to deadly force?? If I were an innocent bystander and felt threatened by the officer, am I justified in killing him? What makes the officers life or his/her feeling of threat greater or more important than those of any other bystander? Ultimately, the question essentially comes down to whether or not there is enough evidence to disprove the officer's story that he/she was defending him/herself or protecting the public. According to Georgia Fevrell "Society has put it into our heads that the officer is always right". This thinking "most assuredly must change".

3. LACK OF POLICE ACCOUNTABILITY FOR KILLING UNARMED BLACKS

Moreover, one other case in which a sheriff deputy said that he shot an unarmed suspect who grabbed for his gun; the autopsy report, told a different story. A person is not shot four times in the back and then claim self-defense. The victim could not have been going for a gun if he/she were running away. Unfortunately, half of the criminal cases analyzed by the <u>Washington Post</u> and researchers at Bowling Green, KY, prosecutors cited forensics and autopsy reports that showed this very same situation; unarmed suspects who were shot in the back. Yet nothing was done to hold the officer who committed the crime accountable for the killings. Even in cases where there was extremely strong evidence of wrong doing by the officer like the case of Sheriff Tim Roberson in South Carolina who killed William Sheffield, a white 45-year-old man wanted for stealing a gas grill and three hauling trailers. Sheffield was gunned down by the deputy who shot him in the back; ONE SHOT WAS POINT BLANK, AN EXECUTION SHOT. The prosecutor stated the forensics evidence was "the strongest of any case in his career". Even though his deputy was indicted on a murder charge, citing the law that forbids an officer from shooting a suspect in the back, the jury acquitted the deputy based on his account of the incident. Even with such strong forensics to the contrary, the officer was not punished for taking a human life. Something is terribly wrong with this picture, and it is systemic. The system has to be changed so that such criminal behavior cannot be allowed to continue to be business as usual. America has been hoodwinked into believing that the officer is always right in spite of what we see and know to be the truth. Another even more stunning acquittal was the Officer Michael Brelo who was charged with two counts of felony voluntary manslaughter in the death of Malissa Williams and Timothy Russell of Cleveland, Ohio. According to records, the deadly encounter occurred when Timothy Russell, 43, and Malissa Williams, 30, drove past Cleveland headquarters on a November night in 2012 and their Chevy Malibu fatefully backfired. Officers mistook the sound of gunfire and went in pursuit. Sixty-two (62) police vehicles chased the Chevy through city streets at speeds up to 110 mph. Cameras captured the pursuit. The suspects later found to be under the influence of drugs, came to a stop in a middle school parking lot. Eleven officers got out of their cars and formed a semicircle around the Chevy, court records show. Although TWO POLICE RADIO BROADCASTS HAD REPORTED THAT THE PAIR WAS UNARMED, THE OFFICERS OPENED FIRE, SHOOTING 139 TIMES. BRELO himself FIRED 34 SHOTS AT THE CAR AND THEN CLIMBED ONTO THE HOOD OF THE CHEVY AND FIRED 15 MORE TIMES "at close range" through the windshield, State Investigation records show.

In a statement to investigators with the Ohio Attorney General's Office, Brelo did not deny firing the shots and he gave the standard fear for his life statement "that he believed gunfire was coming from inside the vehicle. "I've never been so afraid in my life, he said". "I thought my partner and I would be shot and that we were going to be killed." FALSE PERCEPTION! or just an outright lie.

Cuyahoga County Common Pleas Judge John P. O'Donnell ruled "the State did not prove beyond a reasonable doubt that Michael Brelo knowingly caused the deaths of Timothy Russell and Malissa Williams because the element of causation was not proved for both counts". Ridiculous! We are forced to believe what the evidence does not support. Knowingly or not, Brelo murdered those two people. What a travesty of justice and shame on Judge O'Donnell and the laws of the State of Ohio to let such criminal acts by law enforcement go unpunished. Did he not prove that Brelo knowingly caused the victims deaths? How could he have not known that firing through the windshield 15 times was not knowingly and intended to KILL THE VICTIMS! Our nation cannot survive if we continue to allow such brutal behaviors to go unpunished. Clearly any rational, morally, unbiased person would have seen this case differently. Shame on you Judge O'Donnell and the state of Ohio for condoning such inhumane behavior.

SUMMARY PART I

Clearly the evidence and research findings show that there is continued abuse and killing of people generally, and people of color specifically throughout America. Such murders also demonstrate the lack of value that some officers place on the lives of not only people of color, but white lives as well. Without a doubt, the continued murderous behavior of unarmed individuals perpetuates the myth that black lives do not matter and should be taken as less than human.

PART II

FACES OF THE ABUSED

1. PEOPLE OF COLOR KILLED BY POLICE 1999-2014

The following short summaries come from a report by Rich Jazwiak and Aleksander Chan in Gawker 2014 [40]. The information contained herein is not a totality of such incidents, but rather a look at the most glaringly examples of unarmed black people who were killed by law enforcement unintentionally or not, yet clearly not a mistake. The reader is encouraged to examine the vignettes and arrive at your own conclusions regarding such disproportional use of lethal force against one segment of the American population which happens to be black.

Unarmed People of Color Killed by Police, 1999-2014

On Wednesday, after the announcement that NYPD Officer Daniel Pantaleo would not be indicted for killing Eric Garner, the <u>NAACP's Legal Defense Fund Twitter</u> posted a series of tweets naming 76 men and women who were killed in police custody since the 1999 death of Amadou Diallo in New York. Starting with the most recent death, what follows are more detailed accounts of many of those included in the Legal Defense Fund's tweets." [42]

Rumain Brisbon, 34, Phoenix, Ariz.—Dec. 2, 2014

Brisbon, a black father of four, UNARMED and was shot to death when a police officer mistook his bottle of pills for a gun. **Repercussion:** Pending [42]

Tamir Rice, 12, Cleveland, Ohio—Nov. 22, 2014

Tamir Rice was recklessly shot and killed in a Cleveland park while playing with his pellet gun. The officer who killed him opened fire immediately after spotting him in the park. **Repercussion:** The officer who killed Tamir was deemed unfit for a police job by a suburban police department, yet he was hired by Cleveland. No charges were filed against the officer, but he was fired and the Rice family received $6 million in a wrongful death suit. [42]

Akai Gurley, 28, Brooklyn, NY—Nov. 20, 2014

Gurley was shot by Officer Peter Liang in a dark stairwell of a building in an East New York housing project. Gurley was UNARMED. He was called "a total innocent" by Police Commissioner Willian Bratton. A senior police official told New York Times that the cop who was standing behind officer Liang doesn't know what happened; the girlfriend doesn't know what happened either. There is a possibility that Officer Liang doesn't quite understand what happened. **Repercussion:** District Attorney Ken Thompson announced that he is investigating. [42]

Kajieme Powell, 25, St. Louis, Mo.—August 19, 2014

Powell was shot by a police officer who responded to a 911 call, accusing him of stealing pasties and some energy drinks. Cops claimed that Powell approached them holding a knife "in an overlap grip". However, a video footage of the incident shows that he did not go as close to the police, like what they reported and his hands were by his side. Within 15 seconds of arriving at the scene, police shot him. **Repercussion:** Powell's family has filed a wrongful death suit against the St. Louis arresting officers and police chief. [42]

Ezell Ford, 25, Los Angeles, Calif.—August 12, 2014

Ford was shot by police who were conducting "an investigative stop." His family members claim that he was lying down when shot. **Repercussion:** The LAPD, which hasn't closed the investigation, put an indefinite "investigative hold" on the coroner's autopsy report to prevent witness testimony from being tainted. [42]

Dante Parker, 36, San Bernardino County, Calif.—August 12, 2014

Police responded to a call about an attempted break-in where the suspect fled on a bicycle. They found Parker riding his bike nearby. He was UNARMED, resisted arrest and a struggle happened. Police tasered him and he died. **Repercussion:** Pending. The NAACP has called for a federal investigation. [42]

Michael Brown, 18, Ferguson, Mo.—August 9, 2014

Brown was shot by Officer Darren Wilson after an altercation that happened inside his car. Wilson reported that Brown "looked like a demon." **Repercussion:** Wilson was not put to trial by a grand jury. He resigned from the Ferguson police force. According to Brown's family lawyer, Benjamin Crump, "The family greatly wanted to have their unarmed son's killer held accountable. They would look at every legal avenue." [42]

John Crawford III, 22, Beavercreek, Ohio—August 5, 2014

Crawford was fatally shot in Wal-Mart. He was carrying a pellet gun. It was an unsold item and out of its package. A man named Ronald Ritchie told 911 that Crawford looked like he was pointing the gun at people, however, a month later, he admitted that Crawford was not pointing it at people. **Repercussion:** No indictment. [42]

Tyree Woodson, 38, Baltimore, Md.—August 2, 2014

Police say Woodson's fatal gunshot wound was self-inflicted. That would mean that he smuggled his gun into a police station after he was brought there for having several open warrants. According to Baltimore Councilman Carl Stokes, "Things don't seem quite right here. This person could have a gun, a high caliber gun, that could be used against other officers and then he allegedly kills himself." **Repercussion:** Pending. [42]

Eric Garner, 43, New York, N.Y.—July 17, 2014

Police claimed that they saw Garner selling illegal untaxed cigarettes, but witnesses at the scene said he was stopped because he broke up a fight. Officer Daniel Pantaleo placed Garner in a chokehold after an argument. He died of a neck compression from the chokehold along with "the compression of his chest and prone positioning during physical restraint by police." **Repercussion:** The New York City medical examiner adjudicated Garner's death a homicide. Pantaleo was not charged. [42]

Victor White III, 22, Iberia Parish, La.—March 22, 2014

Report from coroner suggested that Victor shot himself while handcuffed in the back of a police car. The autopsy report also claimed that the "victim's injuries were possible to be self-inflicted even with his hands handcuffed behind his back." Such action would have been impossible unless he were Houdini or David Copperfield. **Repercussion:** Pending. [42]

Yvette Smith, 47, Bastrop, Texas—February 16, 2014

Smith was shot to death after she opened the door for officers who were responding to a domestic disturbance call. The officers claimed that she had a firearm, but the sheriff retracted that claim the following day. **Repercussion:** The officer who shot Smith was indicted on a murder charge, and her family sought $5 million in a wrongful death lawsuit. [42]

McKenzie Cochran, 25, Southfield, Mich.—January 28, 2014

The victim was reported to have died of "position compression asphyxia" in a struggle with mall security guards. It was reported that Cochran told them "I can't breathe." The medical examiner ruled that his death was accidental. **Repercussion:** There were no indictments for the security guards. [42]

Jordan Baker, 26, Houston, Texas—January 16, 2014

Baker as killed by an off-duty officer who thought he fit the description of robbery suspects. Both they and he were wearing black hooded sweatshirts. Following a scuffle and a chase Baker who was unarmed was fatally shot. **Repercussion:** The officer who killed Baker was put on administrative leave pending an investigation. Baker's family was considering a lawsuit. [42]

Andy Lopez, 13, Santa Rosa, Calif.—October 22, 2013

Andy was killed by police while carrying a pellet gun that resembled an AK-47. Officers reported that Andy was told to drop the gun. When he turned toward them the officers shot him. **Repercussion:** No indictment. [42]

Miriam Carey, 34, Washington, D.C.—October 3, 2013

Carey unfortunately hit a barricade and a Secret Service officer while making a u-turn at a White House checkpoint. Following a high speed chase, police surrounded her vehicle with weapons drawn and shot her five times. She was UNARMED and died at the scene. Her daughter was fortunately unharmed in the car with her. **Repercussion:** No charges were filed. [42]

Jonathan Ferrell, 24, Bradfield Farms, N.C.—September 14, 2013

After crashing his car in a residential neighborhood, Ferrell knocked on the door of a nearby home. A woman in the house called police who apprehended him and shot him ten times. **Repercussion:** After two grand jury hearings, the officer was indicted on a charge of manslaughter. [42]

Carlos Alcis, 43, New York, N.Y.—August 15, 2013

Following a police mistaken raid of his home in search of a cell phone thief, Carlos died of a heart attack. **Repercussion:** His family filed a wrongful death suit against the city and NYPD for $10 million. [42]

Larry Eugene Jackson, Jr., 32, Austin, Texas—July 26, 2013

The officer fatally shot Larry during a scuffle that resulted from a chase that took place while Larry was trying to "defraud" a bank. **Repercussion:** Officer was charged with manslaughter. [42]

Deion Fludd, 17, New York, N.Y.—May 5, 2013

Police report indicated that a train clipped Fludd as he was chased after dodging a subway fare. Fludd's mother indicated that her son denied this charge before dying from his injuries. **Repercussion:** The Fludd family sued the officer involved, the NYPD and MTA. [42]

Kimani Gray, 16, New York, N.Y.—March 9, 2013

The police fired a total of 11 shots that struck Kimani, who was accused of pointing a revolver at them while they attempted to question him. Witnesses and family stated that Kimani had no gun. **Repercussion:** No indictments for those officers responsible for his death. [42]

Johnnie Kamahi Warren, 43, Dotham, Ala.—December 10, 2012

Warren who was spotted struggling with three other men outside a bar was tased at least twice. When additional officers came on the scene, Warren was arrested. He lost consciousness and died soon after at the hospital. **Repercussion:** The sheriff's deputy was placed on paid leave following an Alabama Bureau of Investigation probe. [42]

Malissa Williams, 30, and Timothy Russell, 43, Cleveland, Ohio—November 29, 2012

After being chased by 62 police cars that ended with 137 shots fired at his car, both Russell and Williams were UNARMED yet killed. Although surrounded at a middle school parking lot, Michael Brelo, a Cleveland officer, climbed on the hood of Russell's car and fired 15 more rounds into the car. **Repercussion:** Each family was awarded $1.5 million settlement from the city. Brelo was indicted May 2014 for voluntary manslaughter. His trial date had not been set at this writing. [42]

Reynaldo Cuevas, 20, New York, N.Y.—September 7, 2012

Reynaldo was shot and killed by police officers as he as trying to run away from armed people who were attempting to rob the bodega where he worked. **Repercussion:** No indictment by district attorney. Family filed $25 million wrongful death suite against city. [42]

Chavis Carter, 21, Jonesboro, Ark.—July 29, 2012

Carter, UNARMED, was detained for marijuana while his supposedly concealed weapon was undetected. He was not suicidal yet officers say he killed himself while handcuffed in the back of the police car. His family/mother indicated that he was left-handed (he would have shot himself with his right hand). **Repercussion:** The family filed a wrongful death suit wile the officers were placed on administrative leave and the FBI came in to monitor the case. [42]

Shantel Davis, 23, New York, N.Y.—June 14, 2012

Davis, an UNARMED woman, was killed by police who chased her in a stolen car through East Flatbush where she crashed. **Repercussion:** Officer who killed her was placed on administrative duty. [42]

Sharmel Edwards, 49, Las Vegas, Nev.—April 21, 2012

The police chased Edwards who was suspected of stealing a vehicle. When she was stopped and able to leave the car, cops said she pointed a gun at them. They opened fire killing her. Three witnesses disputed that claim, and two of them stated that she was not carrying a weapon at all. **Repercussion:** DA of Clark County ruled that officers acted reasonably and lawfully in killing her. [42]

Tamon Robinson, 27, New York, N.Y.—April 18, 2012

Police were called and informed that Tamon was stealing paving stones. When police confronted Tamon, who was UNARMED, he ran toward his mother's place of residence. Police chased him by car and ran over him. **Repercussion:** The Robinson family filed a wrongful death suit against the city and reached a $2 million settlement. [42]

Ervin Jefferson, 18, Atlanta, Ga.—March 24, 2012

Jefferson was killed outside an Atlanta apartment complex by security guards. **Repercussion:** Both security guards were arrested and charged with impersonating the police. [42]

Kendrec McDade, 19, Pasadena, Calif.—March 24, 2012

Two police officers chased and shot McDade to death following a 911 call that falsely reported being robbed by two black men at gunpoint. Both men were UNARMED, yet McDade was shot seven times. **Repercussion:** Officers were cleared of any wrongdoing. The FBI and Office of Independent Review are investigating this case. [42]

Rekia Boyd, 22, Chicago, Ill.—March 21, 2012

An off-duty officer fired an unregistered firearm into an alleyway where four people were standing after the officer claimed he saw a man brandish a gun. One bullet struck Boyd in the head killing her. **Repercussion:** The officer was charged with involuntary manslaughter, reckless discharge of a firearm, and reckless conduct. The Boyd family was paid $4.5 million settlement. [42]

Shereese Francis, 30, New York, N.Y.—March 15, 2012

Following an argument with her mother, Francis who suffered from schizophrenia and was not taking her medication, became very distraught. Her sister called for an ambulance but instead, four police officers showed up and chased Francis through the home. The officers pinned her down as she was handcuffed and she stopped breathing and died later at the hospital. The coroner concluded that her death was the result of compression of her trunk during the agitated violent behavior that occurred earlier. **Repercussion:** Family filed wrongful death charges against police department and the four officers with no indictments.

Wendell Allen, 20, New Orleans, La.—March 7, 2012

A New Orleans police officer shot and killed Allen who was UNARMED, as the officer was executing a search warrant of Allen's apartment for marijuana. **Repercussion:** The officer was sentenced to four years in prison after pleading guilty to manslaughter charges. [42]

Nehemiah Dillard, 29, Gainesville, Fla.—March 5, 2012

Dillard was admitted to Meridian Behavioral Healthcare after showing unusual behavior in a stranger's yard. After allegedly striking a member of the hospital staff, police were called and the officers tased him twice with tasers following an alleged attack on the officers. He was handcuffed and a staffer at the hospital injected him with drugs reported by *Tampa Bay Times*. Dillard died of cardiac arrest. **Repercussion:** No charged filed at this time. [42]

Dante Price, 25, Dayton, Ohio—March 1, 2012

Price was shot 17 times after driving away from an apartment complex where he was told to leave his car. **Repercussion:** The two officers pled guilty to involuntary manslaughter and abduction. They are serving 3 to 11 years in prison. [42]

Raymond Allen, 34, Galveston, Texas—February 27, 2012

Police officers responded to a call from hotel that Allen was repeatedly jumping from a second-floor room. Allen was tased, stopped breathing and later died in hospital. **Repercussion:** Allen's wife filed a lawsuit against the taser's manufacturer, Galveston, and the county. [42]

Sgt. Manuel Loggins, Jr., 31, Orange County, Calif.—February 7, 2012

A police officer shot three times through his car window and killed Loggins who allegedly ran his car into a gate at an Orange County high school while travelling with his two daughters. **Repercussion:** The Loggins' family received $4.4 million in settlement of this murder. [42]

Ramarley Graham, 18, New York, N.Y.—February 2, 2012

The police chased Graham, who was UNARMED, into his home without a warrant and shot and killed in his Bronx home. **Repercussion:** The officer was initially indicted in 201, but the case was later overturned. Graham's mother stated that the justice department would proceed with an independent investigation. [42]

Kenneth Chamberlain, 68, White Plains, N.Y.—November 19, 2011

Police responded to an accidentally triggered life alert of Chamberlain. Chamberlain refused to open his door telling officers that he did not need help. The officer called Chamberlain a "nigger" and broke down his door. The officers stated that Chamberlain attempted to charge them with a butcher knife. They tased and shot him dead. **Repercussion:** No indictments filed. Chamberlain's family filed a $21 million wrongful death suit. [42]

Alonzo Ashley, 29, Denver, Colo.—July 18, 2011

When Denver Zoo security became alarmed over Ashley's behavior, police were called. Upon their arrival, Ashley was tased by officers and stopped breathing. **Repercussion:** Although Ashley's death was ruled a homicide by the coroner no officer was indicted. [42]

Kenneth Harding, 19, San Francisco, Calif.—July 16, 2011

Police stated that Kenneth engaged in a gunfight with them after fleeing a routine Muni fare inspection. Witnesses stated that Harding did not have a weapon. The police Cmdr. indicated that the bullet which killed the victim did not match the caliber used by the police. **Repercussion:** No indictment and Harding's mother filed a wrongful death and civil rights suit against San Francisco Police Department. [42]

Raheim Brown, 20, Oakland, Calif.—January 22, 2011

The police shot Brown five times and killed him during a struggle where he was allegedly attempting to stab officers with a screwdriver. **Repercussion:** No indictments yet. The Oakland Unified School District settled with Brown's parents for $995,000. [42]

Reginald Doucet, 25, Los Angeles, Calif.—January 14, 2011

Doucet was accused of disturbing the peace for arguing with a taxi driver. Police were called and when they responded they found Doucet stripped down, a chase ensued and during a violent confrontation, Doucet was shot and killed. **Repercussion:** The shooting was ruled justified and there was no indictment of the officer who did the killing. [42]

Derrick Jones, 37, Oakland, Calif.—November 8, 2010

Police responded to a neighbor's call which accused Jones of assault. Jones left the scene and when the officers caught him they said that they thought Jones was reaching for a gun. The officers fired nine shots hitting Jones, who was UNARMED, six times. **Repercussion:** There was no indictment of the police, yet Oakland settled with the Jones' family for $225,000. His widow lost a $10 million civil suit. [42]

Danroy Henry, 20, Thornwood, N.Y.—October 17, 2010

The police killed Henry by shooting him through the windshield of his car following a major altercation. **Repercussion:** a wrongful death suit was filed by the Henry family but there was no indictment. [42]

Aiyana Jones, 7, Detroit, Mich.—May 16, 2010

Aiyana was shot and killed when her apartment was raided by a special police response team. After throwing a grenade into the apartment, the officers stated that Aiyana's grandmother grabbed his gun which led to Aiyana being shot. **Repercussion:** The officer was charged with involuntary manslaughter. His first and second trials ended in mistrials.

Steven Eugene Washington, 27, Los Angeles, CA—March 20, 2010

Police reported that Washington approached them on a Los Angeles street and appeared to be removing "something" from his waistband. Washington was shot and killed and no weapon was found on him. Washington was later revealed to be autistic. **Repercussion:** The police chief did not indict the officers and recommended they be cleared of any wrongdoing. A civilian commission which oversees the LAPD did not agree and Washington's family received $950,000 in a settlement with the city. [42]

Aaron Campbell, 25, Portland, Ore.—January 29, 2010

Officers shot Campbell near the front of his apartment after he was reported possessing a gun and being suicidal. The victim was UNARMED, walked backward from his apartment with his hands behind his head and was shot because the officer told him to put his hands straight in the air and he did not comply. **Repercussion:** No indictment of the officer, but he was fired for not following protocol, but later reinstated. The city of Portland settled a civil suit with Campbell's family for $1.2 million. [42]

Kiwane Carrington, 15, Champaign, Ill.—October 9, 2009

The police encountered the unarmed Carrington as they were investigating a suspected house break-in. During a scuffle with Carrington, the officer's gun "went off" and killed Carrington. **Repercussion:** No officer indictment but Carrington's family received $470,000 in a settlement of their wrongful death lawsuit. [42]

Victor Steen, 17, Pensacola, Fla.—October 3, 2009

Steen refused to stop while being chased by police. He was tased, fell from his bike and was run over by the officer and killed. The officer may have planted a gun on Steen after his death. **Repercussion:** The officer was suspended for two weeks without pay. Steen's mother received $500,000 settlement from the city of Pensacola. [42]

Shem Walker, 49, New York, N.Y.—July 11, 2009

Walker, who was UNARMED, was shot and killed as he was attempting to eject an undercover officer from his stoop. **Repercussion:** There was no indictment of the officer, yet the City of New York paid the Walker family $2.25 million in settlement. [42]

Oscar Grant, 22, Oakland, Calif.—January 1, 2009

The police detained Grant along with some of his friends following reports of a fight at a BART train station. A police officer shot Grant while he was lying "face down" for resisting arrest. The officer claimed that he intended to tase Grant. **Repercussion:** The officer was found guilty of involuntary manslaughter and not guilty of second-degree murder and voluntary manslaughter. He received a two- year prison sentence and BART paid the Grant family $2.8 million to settle the civil suit they had filed. [42]

Tarika Wilson, 26, Lima, Ohio—January 4, 2008

Wilson was shot and killed by a SWAT team that raided her home with the intention of arresting her boyfriend for selling drugs. **Repercussion:** The officer who shot Wilson was acquitted of two misdemeanors: negligent homicide and negligent assault. The Wilson family was paid $2.5 million for a wrongful death settlement. [42]

DeAunta Terrel Farrow, 12, West Memphis, Ark.—July 22, 2007

The police officer shot Farrow who was walking with his 14 year old cousin. The officer claimed that he did not realize that the gun Farrow was carrying was a toy until after he shot and killed him. **Repercussion:** The officer was not indicted but resigned from the force. [42]

Sean Bell, 23, New York, N.Y.—November 25, 2006

As Bell and a group of his friends were leaving a scene of mounting tension with police, the police fired some 50 shots into Bell's car which killed him. **Repercussion:** All officers were acquitted of charges. They and their commanding officer were fired and New York agreed to pay Bell's family $3.25 million to settle a wrongful death suit. [42]

Henry Glover, 31, New Orleans, La.—September 2, 2005

Glover was shot by NOPD officer at a strip mall in New Orleans following hurricane Katrina. With the help of a friend, Glover tried to get help and ended up handcuffed and dead. The officer set fire to Glover's body in his friend's car. **Repercussion:** The officer was indicted and sentenced to 25 years and 9 months for manslaughter conviction. His partner was also sentenced to 17 years and 3 months for obstruction of justice. After serving 1 ½ years the first officer sentenced was vacated by the Fifth Circuit Court of Appeals and two years of his partner's sentence. The first officer was acquitted in a new trial. [42]

Ronald Madison, 40, and James Brisette, 17, New Orleans, La.—Sept. 4, 2005

Police responded to a call claiming gunfire on the Danziger Bridge. Upon their arrival, they opened fire hitting Brisette. Madison, his developmentally disabled friend, fled the scene. The two cops chased him down and shot him. The other cop was convicted of stomping Madison on his back before he died. **Repercussion:** As many as five officers were convicted and received sentences between 6 and 65 years on various charges such as conspiracy to conceal evidence. A month later the convictions were vacated and a new trial ordered by the same judge that had convicted them earlier. Such action was highly unusual. [42]

Timothy Stansbury, 19, New York, N.Y.—January 24, 2004

Stansbury was shot and killed by police when he pushed open the rooftop door of a building the police were patrolling. Stansbury was UNARMED. **Repercussion:** No indictment of officer yet NYPD settled a wrongful death suit with Stansbury family for $2 million. [42]

Alberta Spruill, 57, New York, N.Y.—May 16, 2003

Alberta was killed by police acting on a bad information call that indicated there were guns and drugs in her apartment. Police arrived and threw a concussion grenade into her apartment. Alberta suffered a heart attack and died. **Repercussion:** There were no indictments, but the city paid the Spruill family $1.6 million as settlement for a wrongful death lawsuit. [42]

Ousmane Zongo, 43, New York, N.Y.—May 22, 2003

Police were investigating (CD and DVD piracy) and shot Zongo four times (twice in the back) during their raid of the storage facility where Zongo worked. Zongo was unarmed and his business which was art and musical instrument reparation which had nothing to do with what police were investigating. **Repercussion:** The officer was convicted of criminally negligent homicide and sentenced to 5 years probation and lost his job. The Zongo family were paid $3 million in a wrongful death suit settlement. [42]

Orlando Barlow, 28, Las Vegas, Nev.—February 28, 2003

Orlando who was UNARMED, was shot in the back while attempting to surrender to Las Vegas Nevada police. His murder was instrumental in generating the national debate regarding the use of deadly force against unarmed American people. Orlando was watching the children of his female acquaintance. The woman phoned police and reported being held hostage by a man with a gun. Four officers arrived at the residence and convinced Orlando to exit the house. He was ordered to exit the house by walking backwards with his hands in the air. He was ordered to his knees and as the officers approached Orlando one of the officers fired a round which killed Orlando. The officer testified that he saw Orlando reach for his waistband while kneeling and thought he had a gun. **Repercussion:** The killing was ruled "excusable" yet the officer was ordered to be removed from his job. The Barlow family filed a wrongful death suit and were paid $250,000 settlement from the police department. [42]

Timothy Thomas, 19, Cincinnati, Ohio—April 7, 2001

A chase ensued after nine officers ran after Thomas, who was wanted for 14 misdemeanor counts. Twelve counts were for traffic violations. After the encounter into an alley, Patrolman Stephen Roach, who joined the group of nine officers during the pursuit, shot Thomas. Later after the incident, it was revealed that Thomas was attempting to pull up his pants as opposed by Roach's belief that Thomas was going for a gun. **Repercussion:** Roach was acquitted on a charge of negligent homicide. It was later revealed on the investigation that he lied on his incident report and broke protocol. [42]

Prince Jones, 25, Fairfax County, Va.—Sept. 1, 2000

An undercover narcotics agent fired 16 shots at an UNARMED Jones hitting him eight times killing him. The officer admitted he mistook Jones for someone else. **Repercussion:** The Fairfax commonwealth's attorney and the Justice Department decided not to file charges against the officer, Carlton Jones. Price Jones's parents and daughter received $3.7 million in a wrongful death lawsuit years following the killing. [42]

Ronald Beasley, 36, and Earl Murray, 36, Dellwood, Mo.—June 12, 2000

Beasley and Murray were shot and killed during an attempted drug bust in a restaurant parking lot. They were small-time drug dealers as described by their family and friends. One cop called the killings as "unintended, but not a mistake." **Repercussion:** The investigation lasted for a year or so but the officers were acquitted of any wrongdoing. [42]

Patrick Dorismond, 26, New York, NY—March 16, 2000

An undercover cop approached and asked Dorismond and his friend, Kevin Kaiser, where he could buy marijuana while they were standing outside of a lounge. A scuffle ensued and another undercover cop, Anthony Vasquez, came to the rescue. Vasquez claimed Dorismond grabbed his gun causing it to fire into Dorismond's chest. To Vasquez defense, he said he attempted to pull Dorismond out of a confrontation with another cop but without success. **Repercussion:** Vazquez was freed from charges filed by the Dorismond family after New York paid a settlement of $2.25 million for a wrongful death suit. [42]

Malcolm Ferguson, 23, New York, N.Y.—March 1, 2000

Drug officers made an investigation as they noticed some movement in a hallway of a public housing building. Ferguson, who was UNARMED, climbed up the stairs. "At some point, on the second-floor landing, there was a struggle," Chief John Scanlon said. "The [officer Officer Louis Rivera's] firearm discharged." **Repercussion:** Rivera was absolved of misdeed. Ferguson's mom, Juanita Young, received a settlement of $10.5 million for her suit of wrongful death against the NYPD and the city. [42]

Amadou Diallo, 23, New York, N.Y.—Feb. 4, 1999

Four officers in civilian clothes fired 41 shots at an UNARMED Diallo outside his apartment in Bronx. Diallo was hit 19 times. A wallet in Diallo's pocket was mistaken as a gun. The reason the officers initially approached him was that he appears to have matched the description of a serial rapist. **Repercussion:** The Diallo's mother filed for a wrongful death suit against the officers and New York City for $61 million ($20m plus $1m for each shot fired by the officers). The officers were acquitted of all charges. The family was paid a wrongful death settlement of $3 million. [42]

Table 1

Results of Cases Filed Against Law Enforcement 1999 - 2014

No.	Case	Year	Location	Age	Armed (M/F)	Unarmed (M/F)	Repercussion
1.	R. Brisborn	2014	Phoenix, AZ	34		M	Pending
2.	T. Rice	2014	Cleveland OH	12		M	$6M settlement
3.	A. Gruley	2014	Brooklyn, NY	28		M	Investigating
4.	K. Powell	2014	St. Louis, MO	25		M	Filed suit
5.	E. Ford	2014	Los Angeles, CA	25		M	Investigative Hold
6.	D. Parkey	2014	San Bernardino, CA	36		M	Federal Investigation
7.	M. Brown	2014	Ferguson, MO	18		M	No Indictment
8.	J. Crawford, III	2014	Beavercreek, OH	22		M	No Indictment
9.	T. Woodson	2014	Baltimore, MD	38		M	Pending
10.	E. Gardner	2014	New York, NY	43		M	No Indictment
11.	V. White, III	2014	Iberia Parish, LA	22		M	Pending
12.	Y. Smith	2014	Bastrop, TX	47		F	Indicted; $5M suit
13.	M. Cochran	2014	Southfield, MI	25		M	No Indictment
14.	J. Baker	2014	Houston, TX	26		M	Pending investigation
15.	A. Lopez	2013	Santa Rosa, CA	13		M	No Indictment
16.	M. Cary	2013	Washington, D.C.	34		F	No Charges
17.	J. Ferrel	2013	Bradfield Farms, NC	24		M	Indicted/Voluntary Manslaughter
18.	C. Alcis	2013	New York, NY	43		M	Suit filed $10M
19.	L. E. Jackson	2013	Austin, TX	32		M	Indicted/Manslaughter
20.	D. Fludd	2013	New York, NY	17		M	Suit filed
21.	K. Gray	2013	New York, NY	15		M	No Indictment
22.	J. K. Warren	2012	Dothan, AL	43		M	No indictment
23.	M. Williams	2012	Cleveland, OH	30		M	$1.5M settlement (Brelo indicted)
24.	T. Russell	2012	Cleveland, OH	43		M	$1.5M settlement (Brelo indicted)
25.	R. Cuevas	2012	New York, NY	20		M	$25M suit filed; No Indictment

No.	Case	Year	Location	Age	Armed (M/F)	Unarmed (M/F)	Aftermath
26.	C. Carter	2012	Jonesboro, AR	21		M	Wrongful death suit; No Indictment
27.	S. Davis	2012	New York, NY	19	F		No Indictment
28.	S. Edwards	2012	Las Vegas, NV	49	F		No Indictment
29.	T. Robinson	2012	New York, NY	27		M	$2M Settlement; Wrongful death suit
30.	E. Jefferson	2012	Atlanta, GA	18		M	Security Guards arrests/pending
31.	K. McDade	2012	Pasadena, CA	19		M	Investigation pending
32.	R. Boyd	2012	Chicago, IL	22	F		Officer charged; $4.5M wrongful death/ charges dropped
33.	S. Francis	2012	New York, NY	30	F		Lawsuit filed
34.	W. Allen	2012	New Orleans, LA	20		M	Officer charged; 4 yrs. in prison
35.	N. Dillad	2012	Gainsville, FL	29		M	Indicted
36.	D. Price	2012	Dayton, OH	25		M	Indicted 3-11 years
37.	R. Allen	2012	Galveston, TX	34		M	Filed suit
38.	M. Loggins	2012	Orange Co, CA	31		M	$4.4M settlement
No.	Case	Year	Location	Age	Armed (M/F)	Unarmed (M/F)	Aftermath
39.	R. Graham	2012	New York, NY	18		M	No Indictment
40.	K. Chamberlain	2011	White Plains, NY	68		M	No Indictment; $21M lawsuit filed
41.	A. Ashley	2011	Denver, CO	29		M	No Indictment; Suit filed
42.	K. Harding	2011	San Francisco, CO	19		M	No Indictment; Suit filed
43.	R. Brown	2011	Oakland, CA	20	M		No Indictment; $995K settlement
44.	R. Doucet	2011	Los Angeles, CA	25		M	No Indictment
45.	D. Jones	2010	Oakland, CA	37		M	No Indictment; $225K settlement
46.	D. Henry	2010	Thornwood, NY	20		M	No Indictment
47.	A. Jones	2010	Detroit, MI	7		F	Indictment; Mistrial
48.	S. E. Washington	2010	Los Angeles, CA	27		M	No Indictment; $950K settlement
49.	A. Campbell	2010	Portland, Organ	25		M	No Indictment; $1.2M settlement
50.	K. Carrington	2009	Champaign, IL	15		M	No Indictment; $470K settlement

51.	V. Steen	2009	Pensacola, FL	17		M	No Indictment; $500K settlement
52.	S. Walker	2009	New York, NY	49		M	No Indictment; $2.25M settlement
53.	O. Grant	2009	Oakland, CA	22		M	Indicted 2 yr. sentence; $2.8M settlement
54.	T. Wilson	2008	Lima, OH	26		F	No Indictment; $2.5M settlement
55.	D. Terrel	2007	West Memphis, AR	12		M	No Indictment; No settlement
56.	S. Bell	2006	New York, NY	23		M	No Indictment; $3.25M settlement
57.	H. Glover	2005	New Orleans, LA	31		M	Acquitted
58.	R. Madison	2005	New Orleans, LA	40		M	Indicted; Vacated convictions
59.	J. Briscette	2005	New Orleans, LA	17		M	Indicted; Vacated convictions
60.	T. Stansbury	2004	New York, NY	19		M	No Indictment; $2M settlement
61.	A. Spruill	2003	New York, NY	57		F	No Indictment; $1.6M settlement
62.	O. Zongo	2003	New York, NY	43		M	Indicted; $3M settlement
63.	O. Barlow	2003	Las Vegas, NV	28		M	No Indictment; $250,000 settlement
64.	T. Thomas	2001	Cincinnati, OH	19		M	No Indictment
65.	P. Jones	2001	Fairfax County, VA	26		M	No Indictment; $3.7M settlement
66.	R. Beasly	2000	Dellwood, MO	36		M	No Indictment
67.	E. Murray	2000	Dellwood, MO	36		M	No Indictment
68.	P. Drismond	2000	New York, NY	26		M	Indicted; $2.25M settlement
69.	M. Ferguson	2000	New York, NY	23		M	No indictment; $10.5M settlement
70.	A. Diallo	1999	New York, NY	23		M	No Indictment; $3M settlement

SUMMARY PART II

The actual results of the court cases filed against police officers who killed people of color 1999-2014 are quite interesting and reveal information that the general population may be unaware. Five of the court cases that were filed were still pending or being investigated at this rendering. Seven cases had just been filed with no results. Thirty-seven cases that were filed resulted in NO indictment or charges being levied against officers. Ten cases resulted in charges being filed, four cases were still being investigated and twenty-five cases resulted in case settlements that ranged between two hundred twenty-five thousand and undisclosed amounts of up to Twenty-five million. In some cases, settlements were reached with families without indictments, while others received settlements with indictments. It is noteworthy that 37 cases almost 53 percent were dismissed with no charges, settlements of indictments. 21 cases or 30 percent of the cases received cash settlements either with or without indictments. These data seem clearly to illustrate that there are serious issues with our justice system regarding accountability of law enforcement for killing people of color throughout America.

PART III

I FEARED FOR MY LIFE SAFETY NET

1. ARE SHOOTING/MURDERS EVER JUSTIFIED?

An important question that requires immediate attention is "Were the officers who used deadly force justified in their actions; and to what extent did the race of the victim have an impact on the decision of the officer to kill the person"? Clearly, all are aware of the hazards and dangers involved in police work and the need to make life and death decisions in split seconds. Unfortunately, in too many fatal shootings, the officer need only to indicate that he or she feared for their life or the safety of others prior to using deadly force to be exonerated from punishment for such horrible acts. Even when investigations and videos show no imminent threat to the officer, the decision to kill an unarmed human being is made far too often. Indeed, there needs to be serious consequences for such murders as well as immediate disclosure of all evidence to the public in order to avoid any perception of police collusion to synchronize their stories before releasing information for public scrutiny. Although the outcry by social activists suggests that white officers are 80% more likely to kill a black person than a white person, it is also supported by other research. This information is of little consequence; whether the victim is white or black should make little difference. The more important fact is that a human life has been taken needlessly and there is little to no accountability or punishable consequences for the senseless killing of an innocent human being.

Accepting statements such as "I feared for my life" when the victim is running away from the officer, or is seated in a car as the officer gets on the hood of the vehicle and fires multiple rounds through the windshield at the occupants, and it was determined that there was uncertainty or it was unclear if the officers' rounds were the actual killing shots can no longer be tolerated and accepted. Please stop insulting our intelligence! Are we actually sanctioning such behavior from law enforcement? Yes is the emphatic answer and a **concomitant statement in that it is OK to commit such murders against our citizens generally and blacks particularly.**

Futhermore, the slogan "It is better to be judged by twelve than be carried by Six" is part and parcel that seems to encourage such killings when in doubt, because the office either consciously or unconsciously knows that the system is designed to protect him/her from suffering any real dire consequences for such malicious actions. Much of the debate on the criminal liability of police officers involved in such killings and the role local grand juries play in the shielding of these police officers from criminal prosecution needs to be changed.

It is also noteworthy that the entire grand jury system is anathema to fairness and justice in America. Grand juries have now been banished in all nations except the United States and Liberia. Overtime, the grand jury has become a one-sided force that favors only the prosecution. Defense counselors are not permitted to appear inside the grand jury which has become a secret chamber that allows no adverse party to challenge the TRUTH or CREDIBILITY of witnesses through cross-examination. There are no enforceable rules of evidence during such proceedings which suggest that otherwise inadmissible hearsay is perfectly acceptable. Also, prosecutors are able to offer only incriminating evidence to the exclusion of exculpatory evidence. Indeed, in too many instances grand jurors rubber-stamp a prosecutor's directions. Thus, validating the saying that it is possible to get the GRAND JURY TO INDICT A HAM SANDWICH.

2. CIVIL RIGHTS VIOLATION AND UNCONSTITUTIONAL ACTS

Although grand juries are utilized throughout most of the United States, they are not the only legal mechanism for holding police officers and other governmental officers accountable according to Dodd [34]. Additionally, it is virtually impossible to successfully hold police officers accountable in federal courts for constitutional rights violation of our citizens under 42 U.S. C. ss 1983 of the federal courts for constitutional rights violation, (Section 1983 is a provision in the United States Code devised from the Civil Rights Act of 1871 that allows individual plaintiffs to sue government officials acting "under color of law" to violate rights protected by the constitution and laws of the United States 42 U.S.C. ss 1983).

Since its role in upholding the rule of law in the United States is crucial, this category of civil rights litigation that targets governmental constitutional violations has received far less attention from political science researchers; perhaps because the laws, and the constitutional torts, were developed exclusively by federal judges in an extremely complicated and technical doctrinal framework [34].

Although the families of Eric Brown and Michael Brown became part of a long list of plaintiffs to file litigation under section 1983, according to Chemerinsky [31], New York Times— "How the Supreme Court Protects Bad Cops" their prospects for success have been hindered by recent Supreme Court decisions that undermined the ability of plaintiffs to hold officers and other governmental officers responsible for their unconstitutional acts. Among the most recent ruling that favored the police was Plumhoff vs Richard decided on May 27 found that even egregious police conduct is not EXCESSIVE FORCE in violation of the Constitution [31]. In short, the Rehnquist and Robert court decisions have displayed an increasingly hostile view of section 1983 litigation. Also, a number of cases from the 1970s and 1980s that structured Section 1983 doctrine in a manner that makes it difficult for plaintiffs to successfully sue the police or other governmental officials [34] for such gestapo and brutal acts against our citizenry, many of whom happen to be people of color.

Furthermore, Dodd [34] also suggested that the fate of litigation under section 1983 in the age of Obama was unlikely to meet with success due to Obama's lack of effort to respond directly to these doctrinal developments. The President exemplified an across-the-board lack of enthusiasm with rights revolution's reliance on private enforcement of adversarial legalism. Clearly Obama preferred to use enforcement via the justice Department actions which were woefully inadequate since most civil rights enforcement occurs through civil rights litigations. Dodd [34] further asserts that such an approach is insufficient, since most civil rights enforcement occurs through private civil rights litigation. Clearly, the literature shows that Section 1983 litigation is by far the most important vehicle for the enforcement of constitutional rights violations against police officers and other governmental officials that plaintiffs currently have at their disposal to counteract such constitutional rights violation even with its difficulty of enforcement.

3. WHERE ARE WE AS A NATION

It is ironic that more than 50 years after the passage of the Civil Rights Act, black people are once again in the streets holding signs asserting their basic humanity, reminding a forgetful nation that black lives matter. The fact that these words still need to be uttered speaks volumes regarding where our nation stands at this moment in our history. Just as lynchings were not the only thing wrong with the old Jim Crow system, but merely the ugliest most frightening reflections of it. Today's police killings reflect the unrelenting punitiveness of a new system or racial and social control in this country, a new Jim Crow. Police killings of unarmed black men are not an isolated problem, they are the logical outcome of a system predicated on the notion that some lives simply don't matter. Thus, my assessment is that we still have much work to do in the country in order to approach achieving Dr. King's dream. As we continue to move forward, it is essential that we declare and specify our true identity as a nation.

4. WHAT IS OUR IDENTITY AS A NATION

I didn't just grow up, I was taught to speak when I entered a room; say please and thank you; to have respect for my elders and to get off my lazy rear end and let the elder in the room have my chair; say "yes sir," and "no sir;" lend a helping hand to those in need; hold the door for the person behind me; say excuse me when needed and to love people for who they are and not for what they look like, or what I can get from them. I was also taught to treat people the way I wanted to be treated.

How about you? If you were raised this way say "Amen" to yourself. I contend that we have much work to do with our mentoring for young people as well as our parenting skills, in order to develop a sense of pride and dignity in and among our younger generation.

The pervasive injustices that continue to occur from law enforcement in Missouri a la Michael Brown, 2014, Eric Garner, 2014 in New York, Trayvon Martin, Florida 2013, and of course

Rodney King in California, 1991, continue to demonstrate a lack of value for human life generally and black men's lives in particular. What does law enforcement stand for? What is law enforcement's identity? Do people deserve to die for crimes they commit? A more interesting question is does law enforcement/policemen have a right to kill our innocent citizens who are suspected of criminal behavior? We know that 1 out of 9 persons executed in the USA is exonerated, 1 of 9 is innocent, defined by error. Do you think the FAA would allow commercial airlines to operate with a tract record of 1 out of every 9 flights crashing??? Certainly not!

There is power in identify – what one stands for is very important. Good teachers are needed. Compassionate teachers are essential. A good doctor is a plus. A caring doctor may work miracles. In short, caring and compassionate individuals can get people to do things that others may not be able to get them to do. This axiom also applies to law enforcement. Where is the compassion for our people?

In 1972, our Criminal Justice System in the USA had 300K individuals. In 2012, there were 2,300,000 with another 7 million on probation. The USA has the largest Penal System in the world. What does this statistic reflect about the USA?

In some states 1 out of 3 black men is in jail, or on probation. Justice in America is stated by race, and wealth certainly shapes outcomes **(It is better to be wealthy and guilty in our Criminal Justice System, than to be poor and innocent?)**. Shameful to say the least, and is a terrible negative mark on our nation.

Moreover, because of the war on drugs, mandatory sentences, and the "3 strikes against you" law, 34% of black people in some states have permanently lost their right to vote [38]. By 2020, their disenfranchisement will be higher than before the passing of the Voters Right Act of 1965. We cannot ignore these numbers, yet the nation continues to do so. The country has insulated itself from this significant issue. If you listen, we are told by mass media that the 9/11 tragedy began the first acts of terror in America. Unfortunately, this like many other stories is untrue! Terror in America began during reconstruction, the lynchings, shootings, bombing and other forms of killing, and destroying the property of black people existed in our communities long before 9/11. There is truly a real disconnect here and there is a need for truth and reconciliation, not only regarding terror in America, but also with the death penalty, racism and disenfranchisement in America as it relates to all Americans.

There is no death penalty in Germany. Given its history of the Holocaust and the killing of Jewish people, such acts are considered unconscionable. Not so in America!

Blacks are 22 times more likely to get the death penalty than whites, even with our nation's history of slavery and disenfranchisement of the poor and disadvantaged. We cannot become fully human unless we deal with the difficult issues in our society and our lives. There is a significant need to be more committed to creating hope in America rather than division which seems to be the goal of our government at this time. There is a tremendous need for reconciliation between the mind of our nation and the heart of it. Again, the power of identity. America needs to pay more attention to injustice, disenfranchisement, the death penalty, and the reduction of mandatory prison sentences for drug abuse in our society than to tax deductions for the wealthy. To do this our nation needs to be brave, brave, brave, especially when it comes to acknowledging that race is a major factor in determining how police react to individuals throughout America and that it is intricately involved in all aspects of human activity in these United States of America.

Thusly, human dignity must be respected by law enforcement:

THE CHARACTER OF A NATION CAN BE JUDGED
BY HOW IT TREATS THOSE WHO ARE POOR, AS
WELL AS THOSE WHO ARE DISENFRANCHISED.

Unfortunately, my contention is that America receives very low marks in these areas as demonstrated by our treatment of our Mexican neighbors who were refused entry into the US recently by sending thousands of military troops to the Mexican border to repel their entry. Instead of such belligerence toward our neighbors to the south, we need a commitment of compassion and justice from all law enforcement. Recent killings of unarmed black men nationwide clearly amplifies the need for such as well.

Moreover, we have to be cognizant of the fact that the only purpose of the grand jury is to determine if there is sufficient evidence to bring changes for a felony offense, nothing more. If a person is killed by law enforcement or anyone else, why is that not sufficient evidence enough for changes to be filed against the assailant? Grand juries in my view need to be abandoned totally. They have not served any of our people very well. In most instances they have been the antithesis of helpful.

5. BLACK LIVES MATTER MOVEMENT?

A recent study by MacDonald [30] suggested that movements such as Black Lives Matter protests and the political sympathy that accompanies such efforts, have created an environment where law enforcement officials believe that defiance and hostility displayed by assailants toward law enforcement appears to be the new norm. The study further cites an example where an officer was slammed to the ground and beaten, but refused to shoot his attacker for fear of community backlash. The officer stated that he chose not to shoot because he didn't want his/her family or department to have to go through the scrutiny the next day on national news. It is critically important for all who hear or read about this and similar incidents to recognize that the impact of such reports changes the focus from law enforcement committing murders of unarmed citizens to one that continues to blame citizens for reacting to such matters due to unlawful killings by law enforcement in the first place. Such reports continue to help police departments in America avoid addressing the difficult question of how to fix the racism that continues to exist nationally among law enforcement departments. This is a clever strategy that no longer works and has to be corrected.

Moreover, this is a common conservative narrative which suggests that the disproportionate incarceration rates of black people is not the result of systemic racism, but rather of shortcomings within the black community.

6. DO BLACK PEOPLE COMMIT MORE CRIMES?

It is not uncommon to hear the supposedly neutral comment that "black people commit more crimes than white people." This "fact" according to Kim Farbota 2018 [33] is used to justify a belief that black people have a natural propensity, or that a "cultural of violence," is to blame for problems faced by black people in America. The fact that black people are incarcerated five times as frequently as white people does not mean that black people commit five times as many crimes. Here is why according to Farbota [33].

(1) If a black person and a white person each commit a crime, the black person is more likely to be arrested.

Black people, more often than white people, live in dense urban areas. Dense urban areas are more heavily policed than suburban or rural areas. When people live in close proximity to one another, police can monitor more people more often. In more heavily policed areas, people committing crimes are caught more frequently. This could help explain why, for example, black people and white people smoke marijuana at similar rates, yet black people are <u>3.7 times</u> as likely to be arrested for marijuana possession. (The discrepancy could also be driven by overt racism, more frequent illegal searches of black people, or an increased willingness to let non-blacks off with a warning.)

(2) When black people are arrested for a crime, they are convicted more often than white people arrested for the same crime.

An arrest and charge does not always lead to a conviction. A charge may be dismissed or a defendant may be declared not guilty at trial. Whether or not an arrestee is convicted is often determined by whether or not a defendant can afford a reputable attorney. The interaction of poverty and trial outcomes could help explain why, for example, while black defendants represent about 35% of drug arrest, <u>46% of those convicted</u> of drug crimes are black. (This discrepancy could also be due to racial bias on the part of judges and jurors.)

(3) When black people are convicted of a crime, they are more likely to be sentenced to incarceration compared to whites convicted of the same crime.

When a person is convicted of a crime, a judge often has discretion in determin- ing whether the defendant will be incarcerated or given a less severe punishment such as probation, community service, or fines. One study found that in a particular region blacks were incarcerated for convicted felony offenses 51% of the time while whites convicted of felonies were incarcerated 38% of the time. The same study also used an empirical approach to determine that race, not confounded with any other factor, was a key determinant in judges' decisions to incarcerate.

Farbota [33] concludes that regardless of the exact factor behind the incarceration gap, it is not some neutral statistical fact that black people commit more crimes. The gap is the result of numerous interacting factors, not the least of which is racism. Explanations of the incarceration gap as a result of black criminal propensity or insular cultural deficiencies are critically flawed and by definition racist.

SUMMARY PART III

Inspite of efforts by law enforcement, the media and other governmental agencies to change the focus away from the actual reasons behind the disproportionate number of incarcerated blacks, much of the research and thinking of activists and scholars validates the belief that race and racism seems to play a major role in ALL police, court, and other judicial decisions across America. Nothing positive will change until the nation as a whole recognizes this is a problem that impacts all situations in the USA, and commits itself to addressing the issue. There is no time for denying this factor anymore. We have to address the race bigotry, and hate at the national level, not just in small pockets of America. It is time to pay the piper.

PART IV

CONSIDERATIONS FOR CHANGE
AND IMPROVEMENT

1. WHERE DO WE GO FROM HERE?

As a result of information offered in previous sections, the following suggestions are provided with the hope that they may lead to significant changes in law enforcements use of lethal force in our country. Such change is only possible if America is seriously willing to accept the need for positive change and is willing to take the appropriate steps to change for the better.

To begin, it is essential that an independent council be established to review ALL use of lethal force cases wherever they occur in America. All deadly lethal force cases should be mandated to this council for critical review and recommendations. Improved selections and training for all police officers that would include 2 years of college as a minimum to become an officer of the law nationwide.

2. USE OF THE GRAND JURY HOAX

Another essential change would be to eliminate the use of the grand jury system throughout the USA. America is one of only two common law jurisdictions in the world along with

Liberia that [1,2] continues to use the grand jury to screen criminal indictments according to Wikipedia (2017).

Futhermore, a grand jury may issue an indictment for a crime, also known as a "true bill" only if it finds based upon the evidence that has been presented to it, that there is probable cause to believe that a crime has been committed by a criminal suspect. Unlike an appellate jury, which resolves a particular civil or criminal case, a grand jury court of twelve to twenty-three members who serve as a group for a set period of time in all or many of the cases that come up in the jurisdiction, generally under the supervision of a federal U. S. attorney, the County district (Wikipedia P. #1) attorney or a state attorney general. They hear evidence ex parte / without suspect or person of interest involvement in the proceedings.

While all states in America have provisions for grand juries [3] only half of these states actually use them [4] and twenty-two require their use, to varying degrees [5].

The modern trend is to use an Adversarial Preliminary Hearing before the trial court judge, rather than grand jury, in the screening role of determining whether there is evidence establishing probable cause that a defendant committed a serious felony before that defendant is required to go to trial and ask for a consensus on those charges. In addition, California, Florida, [6] and a few other states [7, 89] also use civil grand juries, investing grand juries, or the equivalent to oversee and investigate the conduct of government institutions, in addition to dealing with criminal indictments.

Moreover, grand jury proceedings are <u>SECRET</u>. The proceedings are generally led by a prosecutor and there is no judge present. The defendant has no right to present his/her evidence or in many instances to be informed of the proceedings at all. The case for such secrecy has been upheld unanimously by the Burger Court in Douglas Oil Co. of CA vs Petrol Steps Northwest, 441 US 211 (1979) [10A, 10B].

Additionally, the Fifth Amendment to the U.S. Constitution provides that "No person shall be held to answer for a capital, or otherwise infamous crime, unless on a presentment or indictment of a grand jury except in cases arising in the land or naval forces, or in the Militia, when in actual service in time of war or public danger......" [12]

A grand jury may be presented with a bill of indictment, before or after a warrant of arrest on an indictable charge, at the discretion of a district attorney. He or she then presents evidence and witnesses to prove the charge. A grand jury can return a true bill, no true bill or a third option, "pretermitting entirely the matter investigated". This requires nine of the twelve grand jurors to determine if a person should or should not be charged with a crime. [11] A grand jury is sometimes referred to as the passive collaborator of a prosecutor or a "rubber stamp" for an indictment, especially if simple acceptance of the bill of indictment is returned as a "true bill." If a "No True Bill" is presented by a grand jury, the case is usually dropped. If a defendant is incarcerated, unless there are other charges, a prosecutor declares nolle prosequi, resubmits and indictment with new evidence, or brings charges of a lesser crime then, providing there is no gross oversight, the defendant is released. The theory is that if a prosecutor cannot obtain a true bill, presenting the prosecutorial evidence with no defensive rebuttal, then a conviction is not likely. [12] Clearly, the decision of the grand jury to indict or not to indict is totally determined by the prosecutor and his/her bias for or against law enforcement officers that determines the outcome. ONE INDIVIDUAL SHOULD NOT HAVE SUCH POWER WHEN AN INNOCENT PERSON HAS BEEN KILLED BY USE OF DEADLY FORCE BY AN OFFICER. There has to be accountability for such reckless killings, which is additional reason to abandon the use of grand juries as presently constituted.

In addition to the above concern, the most persistent criticism of grand juries is that jurors are not a representative sampling of the community, and are not qualified for jury service, in that they do not possess a satisfactory ability to ask pertinent questions, or sufficient understanding of local government and the concept of due process. [14] Unlike potential jurors in regular trials, grand jurors are not screened for bias or other improper factors. They are rarely read any instruction on the law, as this is not a requirement; **their job is only to judge on what the prosecutor has or has not produced**. The prosecutor drafts the charges and decides which witnesses to call. [4] Such decisions are clearly influenced by the prosecutors bias in favor or against law enforcement and is another example of the short comings of the grand jury process and demonstrates additional reasons to discontinue its further use. Also, the prosecutor is not obliged to present evidence in favor of those being investigated. [38]

Individuals subject to grand jury proceedings do not have a Sixth Amendment Constitutional right to counsel in the grand jury room, [16] [17] nor do they have a Sixth Amendment right to confront and cross-examine witnesses. Additionally, individuals in grand jury proceedings can be charged with holding the court in contempt (punishable with incarceration for the remaining term of the grand jury) if they refuse to appear before the jury. [4] Media coverage is not allowed. [18] Futhermore, all evidence is presented by a prosecutor in a cloak of secrecy, as the prosecutor, grand jurors, and the grand jury stenographer are prohibited from disclosing what happened before the grand jury unless ordered to do so in a judicial proceedings. [4]

In 1974 the Supreme Court of the United States held in U.S. v. Calandra that "the exclusionary rule in search-and-seizure cases does not apply to grand jury proceedings because the principal objective of the rule is 'to deter future unlawful police conduct,' [19] and 'it is unrealistic to assume that application of the rule to grand jury proceedings would significantly further that goal." [19]. Illegally obtained evidence, therefore, is admissible in grand jury proceedings, and the Fourth Amendment's exclusionary rule does not apply.

According to the American Bar Association (ABA), the grand jury has come under increasing criticism for being a mere "rubber stamp" for the prosecution without adequate procedural safeguards. Critics argue that the grand jury has largely lost its historic role as an independent bulwark protecting citizens from unfounded accusations by the government. [20] Grand juries provide little protection to accused suspects and are much more useful to prosecutors. Grand juries have such broad subpoena power that they can investigate alleged crimes very thoroughly and often assist the prosecutor in his or her job. They sometimes compel witnesses to testify without the presence of their attorneys. Evidence uncovered during the grand jury investigation can be used by the prosecutor in a later trial. Grand jurors also often lack the ability and knowledge to judge sophisticated cases and complicated federal laws. This puts them at the mercy of very well trained and experienced federal prosecutors. Grand jurors often hear only the prosecutor's side of the case and they are usually persuaded by them. Grand juries almost always indict people on the prosecutor's recommendation. [21]. A chief judge of New York State's highest court, Sol Wachtler, once said that grand juries were so pliable that a prosecutor could get a grand jury to "indict a ham sandwich." [22] And William J. Campbell, a former federal district judge in Chicago, noted "Today, the grand jury is the total captive of the prosecutor who, if he is candid, will concede that he can indict anybody, at any time, for almost anything, before any grand jury." [23] Such power is totally unacceptable in today's world, and must change due to the increased number of unindicted officers who murder unarmed people throughout our nation.

2014 police incidents

The grand jury system in the United States came under renewed criticism following three high-profile cases in 2014, where police officers caused the deaths of Michael Brown, Eric Garner, and Tamir Rice, all of whom were unarmed at the time they were killed. In all three cases, the grand juries voted not to return indictments, despite concerns that the officers involved had failed to follow proper police procedure. [24] The grand jury decisions sparked protests across the United States [25] and further demonstrates the need for discarding this antiquated judicial process.

Due to the criticism against the federal grand jury system [26] there are some reform efforts which include the following proposals: [26]

- Better instructions from judges to jurors about the grand jury's powers and its independence from prosecutors
- Increased access to grand jury transcripts for suspects who are eventually indicted
- Expanded safeguards against abuse of witnesses, including education about their rights and the presence of their attorneys
- Notification of targets of investigations that they are targets
- Optional rather than mandatory appearances by targets of investigations
- An end to the requirement that grand jurors be informed that the defense was not represented in the hearing.

Besides the above stated reform proposals, the National Association of Criminal Defense Lawyers (NACDL) established the *Commission to Reform the the Federal Grand Jury*, a bi-partisan, blue-ribbon panel that included current and former prosecutors, as well as academics and defense attorneys. The unanimous conclusions and proposals of this diverse group were contained in the publication *Federal Grand Jury Reform Report & 'Bill of Rights'*. [27] Among the reforms detailed in that report were the right to counsel for grand jury witnesses who are not receiving immunity, an obligation to present evidence which may exonerate the target or subject of the offense, and the right for targets or subjects to testify. [20]

Finally, researchers Erin Crites, Jon Gould and Colleen Shepard of the Center for Justice, Law & Society at George Mason University studied the experiences of prosecutors, defense lawyers, and retired judges in New York and Colorado. Four key reform recommendations emerged from their *Evaluating Grand Jury Reform in Two States: The Case for Reform* research study included:

- Defense representation in the grand jury room,
- production of witness transcripts for the defense,
- advance notice for witnesses to appear, and
- the presentation of exculpatory evidence to the grand jury. [28]

Also, a 1979 The National Criminal Justice Service (NCJRS) document identifies three steps that could be taken to remove the adversarial role of the grand jury and make them more independent by: (1) giving the target of the grand jury investigation the opportunity to testify; (2) making a grand jury subpoena returnable only when the grand jury is sitting and identifying the general subject area of the investigation; and (3) recording all grand jury proceedings (except the jurors' deliberations), making them accessible for pretrial discovery. [13]

Additionally, it is clear that from the unstinting efforts of prosecutors, lawyers, and academic researchers, that there is enough concern about the effectiveness of grand jurors, there is need to improve/change the Grand Jury process. Yet in spite of such efforts, the overwhelming focus appears to remain on the rights and protection of the defense or perpetrator of an offense/crime committed by law enforcement in the cases described herein. How about the victim who was killed by the use of deadly force? It is criminal in my view to investigate such murders and conclude that the use of deadly force is/was justified when men and women alike had no weapons or instruments that could or would endanger the life of the officer. Such killings are racially based in my view and our legal and judicial system must view and treat them as such. It is unfathomable that such attitudes and behavior are still perpetuated and accepted today by so many in America! It is due time that we cease blaming the victims for being murdered and make law enforcement officers who use questionable unjustified deadly force accountable for their acts of taking an unarmed person's life who in many instances is a person of color. Lawson [32] suggests that the outrage surrounding Trayvon Martin's death was not simply because it was an example of another senseless killing of a young person; but instead much of the anger brought the attention to perceived injustice and lack of apparent consequences for killing a young black (male) teen. This narrative projected a suggestion of racial bias as the unspoken motivation for the prosecutor's initial leniency.

Clearly, this assumption is not wholly without merit as empirical studies have confirmed that race routinely impacts a prosecutor's decision to file or not file charges in such cases. Moreover, one should not forget the purely HUMAN element in the Trayvon Martin case. He was someone's son, and his mother and father grieve his death daily unlike anyone else can. [32] Trayvon was the person being the racialized attribute, the mark of race which is not only disliked but socially dehumanized. A devalued individual whose ability to participate as a full citizen in society is fundamentally compromised by the negative meanings associated with his or her racial status. In essence, a racially stigmatized person becomes socially spoiled, dishonored, and reduced in some minds from the whole and useful person to a tainted, discounted one. [35]

3. BLAME THE VICTIMS

According to Heather MacDonald [30] America's 75 largest counties, which comprise most of the nation's population of blacks constituted 62% of all robbery defendants in 2009, 57% of all murder defendants, and 45% of all assault defendants – but only roughly 15% of the population in those counties. She also states that in New York where blacks make up 23% of the city's population, blacks commit three-quarters of all shooting, and 70% of all robberies according to victims and witnesses. Whites by contrast, commit less than 2% of all shootings in New York City and 4% of all robberies, though they are nearly 34% of the population. New York City crime disparities are repeated in virtually all American metropolies. Such occurrences determine where officers are most often called to a drive-by shooting, or armed robbery, and where officers are most likely to face violent and resisting criminals which can lead to officers own use of deadly force.

Heather's [30] argument seems to suggest that such data points validate or justify all police use of deadly force when dealing with people of color generally and black people specifically. Such thinking is certainly illogical and fails to address or even acknowledge the inherent/overt stereotypical perceptions that such profiling brings to any such situation. Futhermore, when blacks are not robbing or murdering and are running away from law enforcement in _fear_ of their lives, why is deadly force used so often?? Most such victims are UNARMED. Is this related to white racism? No data will ever definitively ascertain this, but we can say without a doubt more innocent unarmed black men and women are killed by white law enforcement than other/all races. This being an undisputable known fact, instead of putting forth justifications for such killings, it is time for <u>ACCOUNTABILITY</u> for such inhumane behavior. I contend that <u>all</u> such cases where an unarmed individual is murdered that the officer stand trial, not before a grand jury, but a group of representative citizens. Then let the chips fall where they may. By so doing, such killings in my opinion will definitely be reduced. Another important consideration is the need for improved training for officers so that they are able to handle tense, volatile situations and not escalate matters by issuing commands to citizens as if they are military commanders. They must be taught to use deadly force as a LAST RESORT, not as a first step to remedy a situation.

Most citizens could care less about following or obeying police commands/ orders when they have done nothing wrong. The problem then lies in the fact that officers have the right to abrogate or take away a person's constitutional rights by issuing such commands that are supposed to be followed. Where is it written that law abiding citizens are mandated to automatically follow police commands when they have committed no crime or feel that they are in no danger or danger to others?? Such commands tend to exacerbate and inflame an already tense situation. This is another example of the need for specific training for officers to assist them with handling such matters WITHOUT using lethal force.

Additionally, research reviewed by Michael Winer [36] shows mixed findings regarding blacks being more targeted in police shootings. Simulation studies conducted in St. Louis concluded that black and white officers were equally likely to shoot African American suspects, while another experiment found that both officers and civilians in simulated situations hesitated longer before firing at black suspects than they did at whites. Such research seems to be flawed because participants lack similar training prior to participation, thus rendering conclusions to be flawed.

Futhermore, any latent or hidden bias or prejudice can be masked because participants know that such situations are not real. There is also research which demonstrates that white people are inherently bias and prejudice toward people of color. [37] Therefore, to suggest or indicate that there is NO relationship between such acts and that racial bias is not a significant factor in police homicides in my view is ludicrous to say the least, as well as disingenuous and disrespectful to an entire group of people.

4. RACISM AND POLICE KILLINGS

Those who criticize the research which maintains racism is a prime factor in law enforcement killings of unarmed blacks indicate that blacks live in high crime areas, which leads to more hostile interaction with police; (more crime = more run-ins with police) which suggest indirectly a justification for use of deadly force by law enforcement.

On the other hand, research by Beer [29] suggests that people, black, brown, white or other confronted by police without any weapon DO NOT DESERVE TO BE KILLED by police gunfire, and argues that even those with a weapon other than a gun, should be able to be apprehended by police without the use of lethal force. He contends further that police should have specific training, skills, and expectations that an encounter, even with a non-cooperative or fleeing citizen, should be resolved by means other than lethal force. Unfortunately this is not the case for a disproportion of blacks in our country.

Another important measure to take is not to allow officers the protected right to be judge, decide/jury, and execute/ administer punishment in stressful situations due to their stating after the fact "I feared for my life," because a suspect or citizen puts their hand in their pocket or out the police sight. In some instances, police promote violence by their demeanor and their overly aggressive approach to citizens. I was taught that law enforcement was supposed to serve, support, and protect us; not intimidate and kill us.

Racial profiling should be made illegal nationwide because of its longstanding and troubling national problem despite claims that the US has entered a post racial era. It is worthy of noting that profiling takes place every day in cities, towns, and large urban areas across the nation where law enforcement and private security target people of color for humiliating and often frightening detention interrogations and searches without clear evidence of criminal activity based solely on perceived race, ethnicity, national origin, or religion. Such profiling violates the U.S. Constitution's core promises of equal protection under the law to all and freedom from unreasonable searches and seizures.

Furthermore, racial profiling alienates communities from law enforcement, hinders community policing efforts and causes law enforcement to lose credibility and trust among the people they are sworn to protect and serve.

5. IMPORTANCE OF VOTING

Blacks and other people of color must use the power of their collective voting rights in **every election** to elect only candidates who support equality and justice for **all**. Data suggests that less than 25% of eligible voters actually voted in recent elections. You know the results, Trump, McConnell, etc. and other conservatives remain in office. It is of utmost importance that people of color unite and support only candidates that are sensitive to the issues and needs of all our communities. People of color must become more proactive rather than being reactive. We cannot wait until another child, teenager, man, or woman of color is killed. The time for action is now. Our leaders need to strive for a new national agenda that includes legislation that will hold all law enforcement and governmental officials accountable for their reckless, and unjust behaviors in such matters.

Additionally, we cannot support or permit our children to continue to be caught up in wearing the hoodies, tattoos, unkempt untidy hair appearance that are so popular among many of our youth today. They must be taught that their image projects too many things that may not be who they truly are as an individual, and encourages stereotypical negative reactions by law enforcement and others. I realize that they should and do have the right to wear hairstyles and dress as they choose, but reality shows us that here and now we are talking about survival, stereotyping, profiling, and life and death of innocent people.

6. STRUCTURAL RACISM AND POLICE BRUTALITY

Other suggestions that may improve the well-being of communities of color, increase national productivity, and create a more equitable society according to Beer [29] are:

- Join scholars to advocate for documenting police related deaths as notifiable conditions so that public health departments can monitor these deaths.
- Support calls for more collaboration and partnerships among commu- nities, researchers, policymakers and law enforcement systems.
- Learn about how structural racism and white supremacy operate within institutions, policies and laws.
- Regardless of your field of work, evaluate whether policies, laws, requirements, guidelines, etc., have unintentional negative consequences for people of color. Similarly, evaluate whether they disproportionately benefit white people and think of ways to level the playing field.

- Advocate for and support criminal justice reform, demilitarization of police, decriminalization of behaviors such as loitering and minor traffic violations, end stop-and-frisk and finally,
- Support movements like Black Lives Matter that raise awareness of police brutality, and help expose and dismantle structural and systemic racism in America.

See Appendix I Limit Use of Force for additional steps to consider for reducing use of lethal force.

SUMMARY PART IV

I find it interesting that when I began this project, I was of the opinion that the injustice that occurs following police use of deadly force in the killing of unarmed black people was racially motivated. I am even more strongly convinced of that opinion now, but more aware of the complexities that always surrounds such killings.

Heather MacDonald [30] in an opinion in the Washington Post (2017) clearly states that blacks constitute 62% of all robbery defendants in 2009, 57% of all murder defendants, and 45% of all assault defendants, but constitutes only roughly 15% of the populations in those areas. She indicated further that in New York, where blacks make up 23% of the city's population, blacks commit 75% of all shootings and 70% of all robberies, according to victims and witnesses. Whites by contrast commit less than 2% of all shootings in New York City and 4% of all robberies, though they are nearly 34% of the population. The implicit or underling question is should police stops, arrests and police shootings mirror population ratios rather than crime ratios? Heather MacDonald [30] maintains that the answer is not forthcoming from the Black Lives Matter activist.

My reaction to the above question is simple. Neither crime ratios nor population ratio will assist with shedding light or solving this significant issue in our nation. By focusing on either set of ratios takes attention away from the lack of accountability for the killing of unarmed black people on one hand and blaming black people for causing their own deaths by fearful law enforcement officers who have a license to kill us on the other. To MacDonald's credit she suggested that the appalling history of racism in this country and the complicity of the police in that history, police shootings of black men are particularly understandably fraught. She states further that police training must work incessantly to eliminate all unjustified uses of police force and make sure that officers treat everyone they encounter with courtesy and respect and within the confines of the law.

Are police bigoted? The fatal shooting of Michael Brown in Ferguson, MO focused attention on the plague of shootings of black men by white police officers. And maybe now, the nation will begin to address the documented racism behind it. Only a fool according to the New York Times would deny that racial bias still pervades aspects of American society. Evidence is clear that some police law enforcement tactics; traffic stops, to cite one example disproportionately target African American/blacks. Also, few doubt that blacks are more likely than whites to die in police shootings; in most cities, the percentage almost always exceeds the African American/black share of the populations. That being said, population ratios are certainly an undeniable statistic, but still fails to address the killing of an unarmed person, usually a black male, without penalty for such brutal and lethal behavior.

I continue to maintain that perception of law enforcement and the percentage of population vs. crime data are both nonsensible because such focus deflects attention away from the real issue; that being the killing of innocent human beings whether white, black or other.

Most killings of black people are done by cops who are white is an undeniable fact. This is non-debatable and needs to be accepted as such. To ask whether race played or plays a role in such killings is fruitless and keeps society in a never-ending cycle regarding racism in America. Since most law enforcement officers are white, it holds to reason that the preponderance use of deadly force will involve them. That however does not and should not excuse reckless use of deadly force. No matter what the officer says regarding fear for his/her life, if no weapon is found on the victim, the officer must be charged and held accountable for taking a human life and in my view punished to the fullest extent allowed by our legal system. Why may I ask is it that there has to be investigation after investigation of the use of lethal force when in many instances there is clear and undisputable video recordings of what occurred. Such videos are acceptable as factual evidence everywhere in our society except in law enforcement use of deadly force!! Why?? Is it possible that law enforcement is seeking reasons to dispute the video and thus exonerate the perpetrator of murder??

When will the legal system stop playing us American citizens for buffoons and when will our government begin to treat all of its citizens fairly and justly, including law enforcement.

The continued blaming of the victim for being killed is waring very, very thin and the bad cops will definitely get their due karma here or in the after world, along with those government officials who have provided shielding protection through legal maneuvers and bad laws such as the Florida stand your ground law. Wake up America, your day of reckoning is in your future and the outcome appears grim.

Finally, if law-enforcement officers were taught to understand that there is a need for them to value and respect all human lives, they may see that most human beings are basically good rather than bad. This seemingly small under-standing might make the difference between a murder and a saved life. In other words, there are few innately bad people in the world, only a few people who commit bad acts.

APPENDIX I

1. POLICY SOLUTIONS

Police should have the skills and cultural competence to protect and serve our communities without killing people – just as police do in England, Germany Japan and other developed countries. In 2014, police killed at least 253 unarmed people and 91 people who were stopped for mere traffic violations. The following policy solutions can restrict the police from using excessive force in everyday interactions with civilians.

2. ESTABLISH STANDARDS AND REPORTING OF POLICE USE OF DEADLY FORCE

- Authorize deadly force **only** when there is an **imminent** threat to an officer's life or the life of another person and such force is strictly unavoidable to protect life as required under International Law. Deadly force should only be authorized after all other reasonable means have been exhausted. (Ex: International Deadly Force Standard; Tennessee Deadly Force Law)
- Require that an officer's tactical conduct and decisions leading up to using deadly force be considered in judgements of whether such force was reasonable. (Ex: LAPD Use of Force Policy)
- Require officers to give a verbal warning, when possible, before using deadly force and give subjects a reasonable

amount of time to comply with the warning. (Ex: Las Vegas Metro PD Policy)
- Require reporting of police killings or serious injuries of civilians. (Ex: The Pride Act; Colorado law)
- Require the names of both the officer(s) involved and victim(s) to be released within 72 hours of a deadly force incident. (Ex: Philadelphia PD Policy)

3. END TRAFFIC-RELATED POLICE KILLINGS AND DANGEROUS HIGH-SPEED POLICE CHASES

Prohibit police officers from:

- shooting at moving vehicles. (Ex: Denver PD Policy)
- moving in front of moving vehicles. (Ex: Denver PD Policy)
- high-speed chases of people who have not and are not about to commit a violent felony. (Ex: Milwaukee PD Policy)

4. REVISE AND STRENGHTEN LOCAL POLICE DEPARTMENT USE OF FORCE POLICIES

Revised police use of force policies should protect human life and rights. Policies include guidance on reporting, investigation, discipline, and accountability and increase transparency by making the policies available online. This use of force policy should require officers to:

- restrict officers from using deadly force unless all reasonable alternatives have been exhausted. (Ex: Philadelphia PD Policy)
- use minimum amount of force to apprehend a subject, with specific guidelines for the types of force and tools

authorized for a given level of resistance. (Ex: Seattle PD Policy)

- de-escalate first. (Ex: Seattle PD Policy)
- carry a less-lethal weapon. (Ex: Seattle PD Policy)
- ban using force on a person for talking back or as punishment for running away. (Ex: Cleveland PD Policy)
- ban chokeholds, strangleholds (i.e. carotid restraints), hog-tying and transporting people face down in a vehicle. (Ex: NYPD Policy)
- intervene to stop other officers who are using excessive force and report them to a supervisor. (Ex: Las Vegas Metro PD Policy)
- have first aid kits and immediately render medical assistance to anyone in police custody who is injured or who complains of an injury. (Ex: New Baltimore PD Policy).

5. MONITOR POLICE USE FORCE AND PROACTIVELY HOLD OFFICERS ACCOUNTABLE FOR EXCESSIVE FORCE

- Report all uses of force to a database with information on related injuries and demographics of the victims. (Ex: Seattle PD Policy; Indianapolis Metropolitan PD reporting website)
- Establish an early intervention system to correct officers who use use excessive force. These systems have been shown to reduce the average number of complaints against officers in a police department by more than 50%. This system should:
- report officers who receive two or more complaints in the past month
- report officers who have two or more use of force incidents or complaints in the past quarter

- require officers to attend re-training and be monitored by an immediate supervisor after their first quarterly report and terminate an officer following multiple reports
- Require police departments to notify the state when an officer is found to have willfully violated department policy or law, committed official misconduct, or resigned while under investigation for these offenses. Maintain this information in a database accessible to the public (Ex: Illinois Law) and prohibit these officers from serving as police officers, teachers, or other governmental employees.

REFERENCES

1. Nestmann, Mark (March 5, 2011). The Lifeboat Strategy (https://books.google.com.co/books?id=mM5VSQ15L78C&pg=PT110&lpg=PT110#v=onepage&q&f=false).Retrieved 1 December 2014.

2. Zapf, Patricia A.; Roesch, Ronald; Hart, Stephen D. (Dec. 4, 2009). Forenic Psychology and Law (https://books.google.com.co/books?id=h0slS-NSCVEC&pg=PA182&lpg=PA182) Hoboken, N.J. Wiley p. 182 ISBN 978-0-470-570039-5. Retrieved 2 December 2014.

3. Brenner, Susan; Lori Shaw (2003). "State Grand Juries" (https://web.archive.org/web/20100718003858/http://campus.udayton.edu/~grandjur/stategj/staeg.htm). University of Dayton School of Law. Archived from the original (http://campus.udayton.edu/~grandjur/stategj/stateg.htm) on 2010-07-18. Retrieved 2010-08-02.

4. "FAQs about the Grand Jury System" (https://web.archive.org/web/20110424124519/http://www.abanow.org/2010/03/faqs-about-the-grand-jury-ststem/). American Bar Association. Archived from the original (http://www.abanow.org/2010/03/faqs-about-the_grand-jury-system/) on April 24, 2011. Retrieved 2011-05-11.

5. Brenner, Susan; Lori Shaw (2003). "Power to abolish Grand Jury" (http://campus.udayton.edu/~grandjur/stategj/abolish.htm). University of Dayton School of Law. Retrieved 2007-03-29.

6. "CURRENT GRAND JURY REPORTS – Miami Dade Office of the State Attorney" (http://www.miamisao.com/publications/grandjuryreports.htm). www.miamisao.com.

7. See, e.g., these 2003 and 2011 grand jury investigation of this type in Philadelphia, Pennsylvania http://www.bishop-accountability.org/reports/2003_09_25_First_Philadelphia_Grand_Jury_Report.pdf http://www.phila.gov/districtattorney/PDFs/GrandJuryWomensMedical.pdf

8. See, e.g., this 2002 grand jury investigation of this type in Westchester County, New York http://www.bishop-accountability.org/reports/2002_06_19_Westchester_NY_Grand_Jury/

9. See, e.g., a new report concerning of civil grand jury investigation in DeKalb County, Georgia on February 11, 2013 http://www.wsbtv.com/news/news/local/judge-refuses-seal-grand-jury-report-burrell-ellis/nWMFK/

10. U.S. Const. amend V.

    10A. Powell, J. and Stevens, J.

    10B. The opinion of the Court and a dissenting opinion, Douglas Oil Company of California v. Petrol Stops Northwest (http://supreme.justia.com/cases/federal/us/441/211/case.html), 441 US 211 (1979), at Justia (http://www.justia.com). Accessed 17 Jun 2013.

11. "16th Judicial District Attorney's Office The Grand Jury Procedure; What vacation may a grand jury take after hearing evidence in a case? #3. retrieved 2009-01-02" (http://www.16jda.com/criminalsystem6.htm).

12. Toncray, Marla (4 August 2013). "Error results in unnecessary jail time" (http://www.maysville-online.com/news/local/error-results-in-unnecessary-jail-time/article_8d54566d-c5d3-534b-8234-4c40ca1b312c.html). The Ledger Independent. Retrieved 30 September 2013.

13. J Shropshire (Fall 1976). "Louisiana Grand Jury – Its Precarious Relationship With the District Attorney: (https://www.ncjrs.gov/App/publications/Abstrct.aspx?id=78462. Southern University Law Review. 6: 151–173.

14. Olson, Bruce T.; Edwards, George John (1973). "Preface by Bruce T. Olson".
In Richard H. Ward. THE GRAND JURY
https://www.webcitation.org/5yrvvEMWN?url=http://www.constitution.org
/gje/gj 1973.htm). Tulsa, Oklahoma: AMS Press Inc. 56 East 13th Street, New York, N. Y. 10003. ISBN 0-404-09113-X. Archived from the original (http://www.constitution.org/gje/gj 1973.htm) on 22 May 2011. Retrieved 22 May 2011.

15. Justice Antonin Scalia. "U. S. v. Williams, 504 U.S. 36 (1992)" (https://www.law.cornell.edu/supct/html/90-1972.ZS.html). Cornell University Law School, Legal Information Institute (https://www.law.cornell.edu/). Retrieved February 15, 2012. External link in | work= (help)

16. Chief Justice Warren E. Burger. "U. S. v. Mandujano, 425 U.S. 564, 581, 96 S. Ct. 1768, 1779, 48 L. Ed. 2d 212 (1976)" (http://supreme.justia.com/cases/federal/us/425/564/case.html). Justicia (http://company.justia.com/about.html). Retrieved February 15, 2012. External link in | work= (help)

17. Chief Justice William Rehnquist. "Connecticut v. Gabbert, 562 U.S. 286, 292 (1999)" (https://www.law.cornell.edu/supct/html/97-1802.ZO.html). Cornell University Law School, Legal Information Institute (https://www.law.cornell.edu/). Retrieved February 15, 2012. External link in | work= help)

18. Gosztola, Kevin (11 May 2011). "2011-05-11 What to Expect in the WikiLeaks Grand Jury Investigation" (https://www.webcitation.org/5ycKns5tH?url=http://wlcentral.org/node/1759). WL Central. Archived from the original (http://wlcentral.org/node/1759) on 12 May 2011. Retrieved 12 May 2011.

19. from the dissenting opinion written by Justice William J. Brennan, Jr. "United States v. Calandra, 414 U.S. 338, 355, 94 S. Ct. 613, 624, 38 L. Ed. 2d 561 (1974)" (https://www.law.cornell.edu.supct/html/historics/USSC_CR_0414_0338_ZS.html). Cornell Law. Retrieved February 9, 2012.

20. "Grand Jury Reform Links" (http://grandjuryresistance.org/reformlinks.html). Grand Jury Resistance Project. Retrieved 7 October 2012.

21. "Grand Jury Clause – 5th Amendment" (http://www.revolutionary-war-and-beyond.com/grand-jury-clause.html). Revolutionary War and Beyond. Retrieved 7 October 2012.

22. "Zimmerman's Bill of Rights" (http://www.nysun.com/editorials/zimmermans-bill-of-rights/87790/). The New York Sun. 16 April 2012. Retrieved 7 October 2012.

23. Campbell, William J. (1973). Eliminate the Grand Jury, 64 J. Crim. L. & Criminology 174, 180 (http://www.nacdl.org/criminaldefense.aspx?id=10372&libID=10345).

24. Dana Ford; Greg Botelho; Ben Brumfield (December 4, 2014). "Protests erupt in wake of chokehold death" (http://www.cnn.com/2014/12/04/justice/new-york-grand-jury-chokehold/). CNN. Retrieved December 9, 2014.

25. Alan Scher Zagier and Jim Salter, Associated Press (November 30, 2014). "Mayor: No severance package for resigned Ferguson officer" (http:/www.reviewjournal.com/news/nation-and-world/mayor-no-severance-package-resigned-ferguson-officer). Las Vegas Review-Journal. Retrieved December 9, 2014.

26. "Grand Jury – Hearsay Evidence: Admissible Before A Grand Jury?, Should The Grand Jury Be Abolished?, Further Readings" (http://law.jrank.org/pages/7199/Grand-Jury.html). law.jrank.org. Retrieved 7 October 2012.

27. The Commission to Reform the Federal Grand Jury: Elkan Abramowitz, Professor Barbara Bergman, Arnold I. Burns, J. William Bill) Codinha, W. Thomas (Tom) Dillard, III, Peter E. Fleming, Jr., Howard W. Goldstein, Frederick (Fred) Hafetz, John

W. Keker, Jim E. Lavine, Gerald B. (Jerry) Lefcourt, Herbert J. (Jack) Miller, Jr., Robert (Bob) Mosteller, William L. (Bill) Murphy, Richard Rosen, David S. Rudolf, Neal R. Sonnett, Brendan Sullivan, William W. (Bill) Taylor, III, Larry D. Thompson, Anton R. (Tony) Valukas, Martin G. (Marty) Weinberg, Theodore V. (Ted) Wells, Jr., Frank Wohl (18 May 2000). "Federal Grand Jury Reform Report and Bill of Rights" (http://www.nacdl.org/criminaldefense.aspx?id=10372&libID=10345). The National Association of Criminal Defense Lawyers (NACDL). Retrieved 7 October 2012.

28. Erin Crites, Jon Gould and Colleen Shepard (November 2011). Evaluating Grand Jury Reform in Two States: The Case for Reform" (http://www.nacdl.org/WorkArea/linkit.aspx?LinkIdentifier=id&ItemID=22943). The National Association of Criminal Defense Lawyers (NACDL). Retrieved 7 October 2012.

29. Todd Beer, Sociology Toolbox (Updated August 24, 2018). "Police Killings of Blacks: Data for 2015, 2016, 2017 and first half of 2018" (https://thesocietypages.org/toolbox/police-killing-of-blacks/). The Society Pages. Retrieved September 2, 2018.

30. Heather MacDonald, Washington Post (July 18, 2016). Police Shooting and Race:
https://www.washingtonpost.com/news/volokh-conspiracy/wp/2016/07/18/police-shootings-and-race/?noredirect=on&utm_term=.df5f581ce3ee

31. Erwin Chenminsky. 2011. "The Conservative Assault on the Constitution." New York:
Simon & Schuster.
________ 2014a. "How the Supreme Court Protects Bad Cops." New York Times, August 26.
________ 2014b. Op-ed: Police Dodge Accountability for Deaths: Orange County Register, December 5.

32. Tamara F. Lawson, St. Thomas University school of Law (Florida) Research Paper No. 2015-04. (November 16, 2017)

"A Fresh Cut in an Old Wound – A Critical Analysis of the Trayvon Martin Killing: The Public Outcry, the Prosecutor's Discretion, and the Stand Your Ground Laws."

33. Kim Farbota, <u>Huff Post</u> (2018). <u>https://www.huffingpost.com/kim_forbota/black_crime_rates_your_st_b_8078586.html</u>. Retrieved October 26, 2018.

34. Lynda G. Dodd, (2015) <u>American Political Science Association</u>, September 2015, Vol. 13/No. 3.

35. Limit Use of Force (<u>https://www.joincampaignzero.org/force/</u>), Campaign Zero. Retrieved January 24, 2019.

36. R. A. Lenhardt, <u>Understanding the Mark: Race Stigma and Equality in Contex</u>, 79 N.Y.U.L., Rev. 803,818 (2004).

37. Michael Wines, <u>Are Police Bigoted?</u> New York Times, August 30, 2014.

38. Chris Mooney, <u>Across America Whites are bias and They don't even know it</u>, <u>Economic Police</u>, December 8, 2014.

39. NY Criminal Procedure Law && 190.05 & 190.25.

40. ACLU. Org. 2018/0 Reasons to Oppose "3 Strikes You're Out."

41. Rich Juzwiak and Aleksander Chan. <u>Washington Post</u> (December 8, 2014) Unarmed People of Color Killed by Police. <u>https://gawker.com</u>.

42. Clay Morton, <u>The Dallas Morning News</u> (November 26, 2013). "Oklahoma officer convicted for fatally shooting unarmed teen."

43. Rich Juzwiak and Aleksander Chan (December 8, 2014) "Unarmed People of Color Killed by Police, 1999-2014." (https://gawker.com/unarmed-people-of-color-killed-by-police-1999-2014-1666672349) The Washington Post. Retrieved June 7, 2016.